W9-APJ-082

What's Blowing In?

CONTENTS

NATIONAL GEOGRAPHIC ■■■ Hampton-Brown

School Publishing

Words with **oa**, **ow**, -**old**

Look at each picture. Read the words.

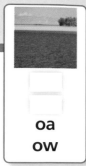

oa
ow

Example:

sn**ow**

bl**ow**

b**oa**t

g**oa**t

c**old**

old c**oa**t

High Frequency Words

air
boy
different
hurry
soon
turn

Key Words

Answer the questions about the pictures.

Two Boys

1. How is each **boy** dressed in a **different** way?
2. Which boy is dressed for cold **air**?
3. Which boy might **hurry** to the beach **soon**?
4. Which boy might see rain **turn** into snow?

What does each boy have?

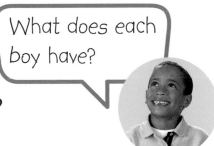

Phonics Games

NGReach.com

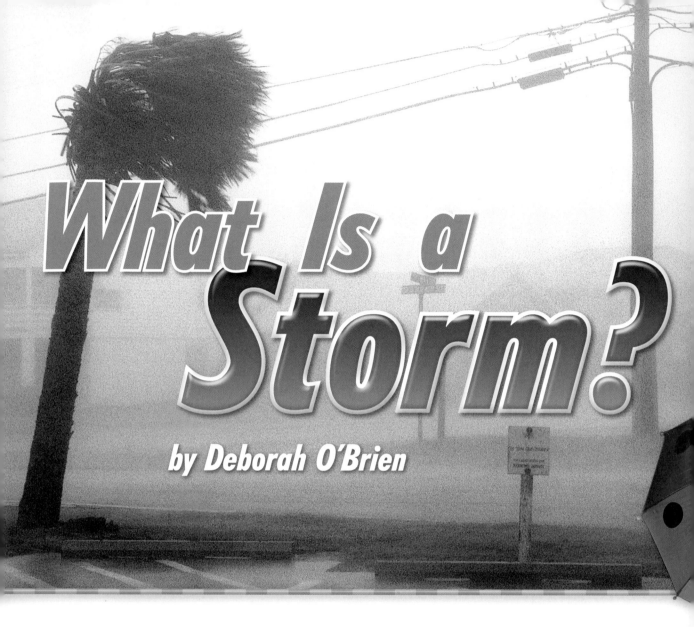

What Is a Storm?

by Deborah O'Brien

What is a storm? A storm is a strong
wind. There are different kinds of storms.
A storm can bring rain or snow.

What will this storm bring?

This storm will bring soaking rain. Look out! There may be lightning in the sky. Just wait! Soon there will be a big bang.

What will this storm bring?

This storm may start as rain. If it gets quite cold, rain may turn to snow. Snow will pile up on roads. Trucks will tow loads of snow.

What will this storm bring?

This storm will bring fast, spinning air.
There will be a cloud shaped like a cone.
It is a funnel cloud. Hurry to a safe
place and hold on!

What will this storm bring?

eye of the storm

This storm has very strong winds and lots of rain. The winds blow over a wide space. In the eye of the storm, the winds go slow. At the edge, the winds speed up. What will the next storm bring? ❖

Words with <u>oa</u>, <u>ow</u>, -<u>old</u>

Read these words.

soak	hold	blow	stick
wind	rain	road	snow

Find the words with the long **o** sound. Use letters to build them.

s o a k

Talk Together

Choose words from the box to tell your partner about the weather.

The _wind_ can _blow_ here.

1.

2.

3.

Compound Words

Look at each picture. Read the words.

Example:

raincoat

snowflake

goldfish

backpack

bathtub

teapot

High Frequency Words

air
boy
different
hurry
soon
turn

Key Words

Look at the pictures.
Read the sentences.

A Different Hat

1. The **boy** needs a hat in the cold **air**.
2. The still air will **turn** into a strong wind.
3. **Soon** the wind blows the boy's hat off!
4. The boy will **hurry** to get a **different** hat.

How is the new hat different?

GO! **Phonics Games**
NGReach.com

15

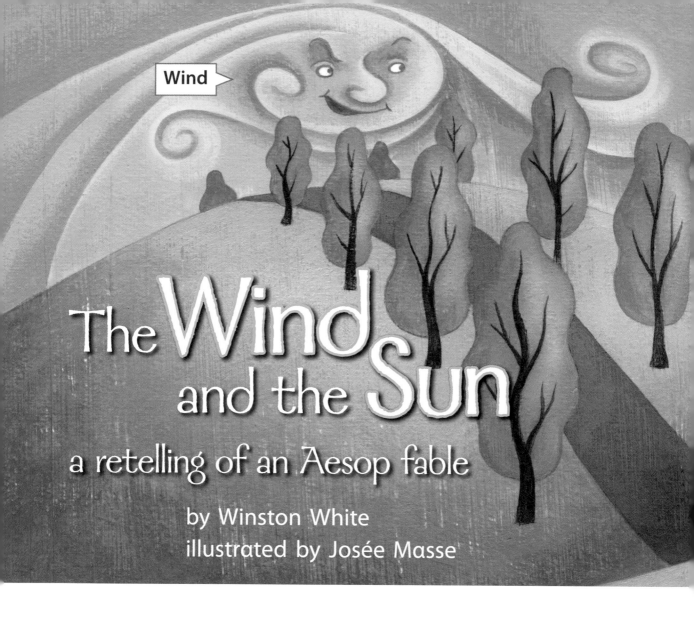

Wind

The Wind and the Sun

a retelling of an Aesop fable

by Winston White

illustrated by Josée Masse

One day Wind said, "I am strong."

"No, I am strong," said Sun.

"How can we find out who is the strong one?" asked Wind.

Sun

Sun said, "See that boy on the road? If you can take off his raincoat, you are the strong one. You may go first, Wind."

Sun hid in back of a cloud. Wind started to blow and blow.

The more Wind huffed and puffed, the more the boy hugged his raincoat close.

The boy started to hurry on the road. Wind went on blowing. The boy did not take off his raincoat.

Wind stopped blowing. The air became still.

Wind said, "I give up. I cannot do it. Maybe you can do it, Sun."

Sun had a different plan. He started
to turn his hot rays on the boy. Strong
sunshine fell on the boy.

The boy did not hurry on the road. He put on his sunglasses.

"Well, that is not in my plan," said Sun. He sent more and more hot rays.

Soon the boy became very hot. He
reached the hilltop and stopped by the
roadside. He tossed off his raincoat.

Wind said, "Sun, you are the strong
one. I am not that strong. You win!" ❖

Compound Words

Read these words.

snowman	wind	raindrops	sunglasses
raincoat	sunshine	snowflakes	hilltop

Find the compound words. Use letters to build them.

r a i n c o a t

Talk Together

Choose words from the box to tell your partner what you can see in the pictures.

I can see the _raindrops_.

1.

2.

3.

Find the Sunshine

Look at the picture with a partner. Take turns reading the sentences. Use your finger to trace the path to the sunshine.

1. First pass the raindrops.
2. Soon you come to the boy in a raincoat.
3. Then you see the snowflakes in the air.
4. Pass the snowman.
5. Hurry to the goat on the hilltop.

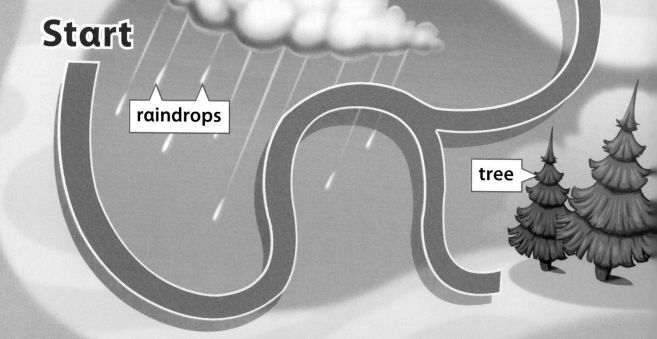

Start

raindrops

tree

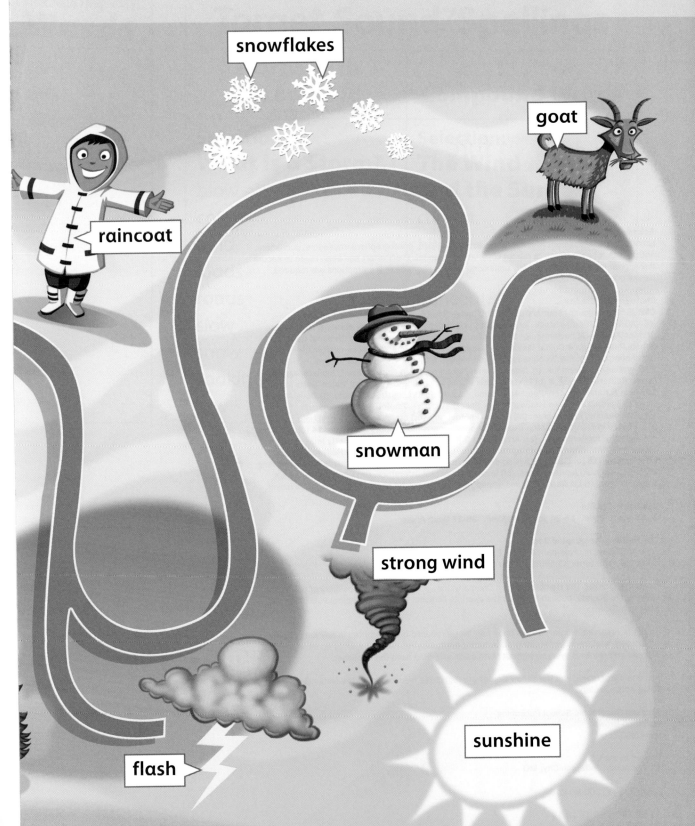